U.S. Presidential Inaugurations

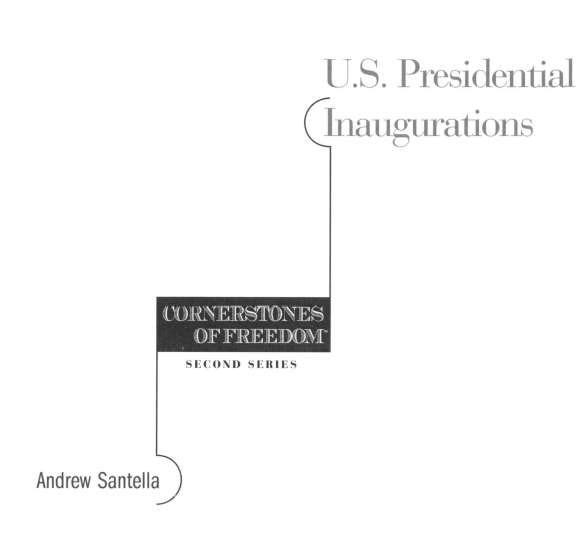

CORNERSTONES OF FREEDOM™

SECOND SERIES

Andrew Santella

Children's Press®
A Division of Scholastic Inc.
New York • Toronto • London • Auckland • Sydney
Mexico City • New Delhi • Hong Kong
Danbury, Connecticut

Photographs© 2002: AP/Wide World Photos: 32 (J. Scott Applewhite), 39 (Robert F. Bukaty); Archive Photos/ Getty Images: 45 top right (David Ake), 27 (Hulton Getty Collection); Art Resource, NY/National Portrait Gallery, Smithsonian Institution: 18 left; Bridgeman Art Library International Ltd., London/New York: 17 right; Corbis Images: 11 (Craig Aurness), 10, 29, 34, 37 (Bettmann), 33, 35 bottom, 35 top; Getty Images: 24 (Frank Fisher/ Liaison), 38 (Bill Greenblatt), 30 (Dirck Halstead), 15 (Liaison), 21 left (Brad Markel), 28, 45 bottom right (News-makers), cover bottom (Mark Wilson/Newsmakers), 13 bottom; Harry S. Truman Library/US Army: 3 background; Hulton Archive/Getty Images: 6 bottom, 21 right, 22 bottom, 41 bottom; North Wind Picture Archives: 8 top, 8 left, 9, 17 left, 18 right, 20, 44 bottom left; Stock Montage, Inc.: cover top, 4, 14, 16 right, 19 right, 22 left, 41 top, 44 top right; Superstock, Inc.: 40, 44 top left (David David Gallery, Philadelphia), 5 top (Metropolitan Museum of Art, New York City), 23 (Jack Novak), 5 bottom, 6 top, 7, 12, 13 top, 16 left, 19 left, 25, 26, 36, 44 bottom right, 45 bottom left, 45 top left.

Library of Congress Cataloging-in-Publication Data

Santella, Andrew.

U.S. presidential inaugurations / Andrew Santella.

p. cm. — (Cornerstones of freedom. Second series)

Summary: Discusses the history and traditions of swearing in the United States President, including inaugural events planned far in advance and those hastily prepared upon the sudden death of a president.

Includes bibliographical references and index.

ISBN 0-516-22533-2

1. Presidents—United States—Inauguration—History—Juvenile literature. 2. Presidents—United States—History—Juvenile literature. 3. Inauguration Day—History—Juvenile literature. 4. Washington (D.C.)—Social life and customs—Juvenile literature. [1. Presidents—Inauguration. 2. Presidents—History. 3. Inauguration Day—History. 4. Washington (D.C.)—Social life and customs.] I. Title. II. Series.

F196 .S26 2002

973'.09'9—dc21

2002001646

1 2 3 4 5 6 7 8 9 10 R 11 10 09 08 07 06 05 04 03 02

IN APRIL OF 1789, NEW YORK CITY was preparing to welcome a special guest. New York was the first capital of the United States, and its citizens were awaiting the arrival of George Washington. Washington was coming to New York for his **inauguration** as the first president of the United States. On the streets of New York, banners flew in celebration. The stairs of Murray's Wharf were covered in red carpeting to greet the guest of honor. A parade of ships waited in the harbor to meet the president's barge. There was just one problem. No one was quite sure what to call the president.

**New York City around 1789,
the year of the first
presidential inauguration**

Today, presidential inaugurations are almost routine. We expect to have an inauguration every four years to start the new presidential term of office. We also expect the president to give a speech, and we expect a parade. But in 1789 no one knew exactly what an inauguration should be like. Even the smallest details had to be worked out. One of those details was how to address the new president.

Even as Washington arrived in New York, Congress argued about what to call him. One member of Congress suggested "His Serene Highness." Another came up with "His

Highness, the President of the United States and Protector of their Liberties." Still another thought these sounded more like titles for a king than for a president. He suggested calling the president simply "Mr. Washington."

This was a problem Congress had not encountered before. It had been thirteen years since the signing of the Declaration of Independence.

George Washington, first president of the United States

· GEORGE WASHINGTON ARRIVES AT MANHATTAN FOR HIS INAUGURATION · APRIL 16.1789 ·

Washington arrives at Murray's Wharf for his inauguration.

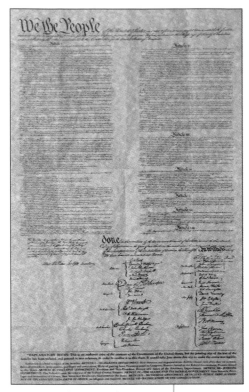

**The Constitution of the
United States of America**

In between, there had been plenty of other concerns. First, a bloody war had been fought with Great Britain to secure independence. Then, there was the problem of devising a democratic system of government that would work. The first government, under the Articles of Confederation, faced so many problems that it did not survive. In 1789 it was replaced by a new system, described in the Constitution.

The Constitution called for a government that would be made up of three branches. The executive branch was to be headed by a president. The Constitution explained how the president was to be chosen. It even provided an **oath** for the president to take when he began his service. However,

A painting of the signing of the Declaration of Independence

The Battle of Lexington was just one of many battles fought with Britain in the war for independence.

it didn't give much detail about how the inauguration was supposed to proceed. And it certainly did not specify how the president was supposed to be addressed.

The crowd that gathered under the balcony of New York's Federal Hall on April 30, 1789 didn't know what to expect. Washington arrived for the ceremony in a carriage. He wore an American-made dark brown suit and

★ ★ ★ ★

THE PRESIDENTIAL OATH

The presidential oath of office reads as follows: "I do solemnly swear [or affirm] that I will faithfully execute the Office of President of the United States, and will to the best of my ability preserve, protect and defend the Constitution of the United States."

George Washington is inaugurated at Federal Hall as the spectators below look on.

The Bible on which George Washington took the oath as president

carried a ceremonial sword. Amid the cheers of the crowd, he made his way up the stairs of Federal Hall to the Senate chamber and then to the balcony. There, atop a table covered by red velvet, lay a Bible. With one hand resting on the Bible and one hand over his heart, Washington repeated the thirty-five word oath prescribed by the Constitution. When he finished, he added, "So help me God." Then he was introduced to the gathered audience as simply "George Washington, President of the United States." The American presidency was born.

* * * *

STARTING THE
INAUGURAL TRADITION

On that day in 1789, the United States was attempting something entirely new. No one had ever formed a system of government quite like the one set forth in the Constitution. No government had ever included a job quite like the president's. In a speech that day, Washington called the American system of government an "experiment entrusted to the hands of the American people." As in any real experiment, no one could be sure of the result. But in many ways Washington set the United States on a course that it would follow over the centuries to come.

He established many of the rules of conduct that presidents still follow today. Even his inauguration became a model for other presidents. Like Washington, most presidents place one hand on a Bible and one on their heart when they repeat the presidential oath. Most say "So help me God" upon completing the oath. Most give a speech at their inauguration, just as Washington did. The first inauguration became the basis for the tradition of presidential inaugurations that developed over the years.

William Henry Harrison, who was president of the United States for only one month

★　★　★　★

Still, no two inaugurations have ever been exactly alike. Most are scheduled to follow a presidential election and are planned far in advance. Others become necessary because of the sudden death of a president. In such a case, the vice president becomes president at a swearing-in ceremony. Most presidents have taken the presidential oath on the steps of the Capitol. In emergencies, however, presidents have taken the oath in hotels or in their family homes. Vice President Lyndon Johnson was sworn in as president onboard a plane.

Even regularly scheduled inaugurations, with all their careful planning, can hold surprises. Some new presidents, such as John F. Kennedy, have delivered inaugural speeches that are remembered many years later. Others gave speeches that were remembered only because they were extremely long. William Henry Harrison's speech, delivered in bad weather, went on so long that it may have contributed to his death exactly one month later.

INAUGURATIONS AND THE CONSTITUTION

Inaugurations usually include parades, speeches, fireworks, and grand parties. None of these events are required by law, of course. The Constitution offered only a short paragraph to guide the planners of George Washington's inauguration. It said that before the **president-elect** could take office, he must promise to do his job properly. A president-elect is a person who has been elected president but has not yet taken office. The Constitution provides the thirty-five-word oath

(or affirmation) that every president of the United States must take. The oath is the most important part of each inauguration, and it is required by the Constitution.

The only other detail regarding inaugurations that is specified in the Constitution is the date of the **ceremony.** Until 1933, inaugurations were always scheduled for March 4. Washington's first inauguration was scheduled for March 4 but was held nearly two months later. According

11

Cold weather delayed Washington's inauguration until April 30.

THE ELECTORAL COLLEGE

The Electoral College is part of a complicated system set forth in the Constitution for selecting a president every four years. Under this system, American voters do not choose their president directly. Instead, their votes are cast for a slate of electors who have promised to vote for a certain president. In other words, when a voter casts his ballot for Candidate A, his vote really goes to the group of electors who have promised to vote for Candidate A. Each state has as many electors as it has senators and representatives in Congress. All these electors together make up the Electoral College. It is possible for a candidate to win most of the Electoral College votes, even though more people cast their ballots for their opponents. This has happened three times—most recently in 2000. That year, George W. Bush won the Electoral College vote, even though more people cast their votes for Al Gore.

to the Constitution, Congress was required to count the Electoral College votes for president and declare the results official. The Constitution also says that Congress can only do business if most of its members are present. But in 1789, cold weather kept many members of Congress from reaching New York City on time. The **tardy** senators and representatives arrived in April—allowing Washington to finally take his presidential oath on April 30.

In 1933, the Twentieth Amendment to the Constitution changed the date of presidential inaugurations from March 4 to January 20. The amendment was designed to shorten the length of time that an

12

outgoing president would serve between the election and the inauguration of his successor. During this period of time the president still in office is called a "lame duck." So the Twentieth Amendment became known as the "Lame Duck Amendment." Before the amendment was passed, a president might be voted out of office in November but would still serve as president for four more months until the new president was inaugurated in March. In 1937, Franklin D. Roosevelt became the first president inaugurated on January 20.

President Franklin D. Roosevelt, whose second inauguration took place after the Lame Duck Amendment

Massachusetts Electoral College delegates take an oath on December 18, 2000

SUNDAY INAUGURATIONS

Inauguration ceremonies are never held on Sundays. When January 20 falls on a Sunday, the official ceremonies are delayed for one day. Sometimes the president-elect will take the presidential oath privately on Sunday. Then he will repeat it in a public ceremony the next day.

John F. Kennedy gives
his inauguration speech.

* * * *

HONORING THE
AMERICAN SYSTEM

Besides meeting the requirements described by the Constitution, inaugurations are also important as public celebrations. In 1961, John F. Kennedy called his inauguration a "celebration of freedom." He was well aware that in some other countries, people had little or no role in selecting their leaders.

Inauguration ceremonies celebrate the choice voters make on election day. They also pay tribute to the system of government established by the Constitution. Consider the participants in a traditional inauguration. The new president is the center of attention at his inauguration, but the Supreme Court plays a role, too. Traditionally, members of the Supreme Court attend inauguration ceremonies. In fact, it has become a tradition for the **Chief Justice of the United States** to read the oath out loud for the president-elect to repeat. However, not every president receives his oath from the Chief Justice. Calvin Coolidge was vice president until Warren G. Harding died of a sudden heart attack in 1923. That made Coolidge president. Coolidge was at the family farm in rural Vermont when he got the news. Because of the emergency, Coolidge's father **administered** the presidential oath.

Senators and representatives also participate in inaugurations. At the first inauguration, George Washington was introduced to Congress before

Chief Justice of the United States William Rehnquist has sworn in many presidents during his time on the Supreme Court.

15

Calvin Coolidge (left) became president after Warren G. Harding (right) died of a sudden heart attack.

WHITE HOUSE INAUGURATION

The Capitol is the traditional site for inaugurations, but it is not the only site. In 1945, Franklin D. Roosevelt chose to be inaugurated at the White House where he stood on the south **portico** to take his oath and deliver a short speech.

taking his presidential oath. Continuing that tradition of respect for Congress, most presidents are inaugurated on the steps of Congress's home, the Capitol building. Since Washington's day Congress has also helped plan inaugurations. Beginning in 1901, a committee of senators and representatives has led the planning for the celebrations. The committee is called the Joint Congressional Committee on Inaugural Ceremonies. Representatives of the armed services take part in planning, too.

Traditionally, the outgoing president participates in his successor's inauguration, too. Even when an outgoing president has lost a bitter, hard-fought election campaign to the president-elect, tradition demands that he help the new president take office. Usually the outgoing president invites the president-elect to meet him at the White House on the morning of the inauguration. The two then travel together to the Capitol for the ceremony.

This tradition dates back to 1837, when Andrew Jackson escorted his successor, Martin Van Buren, to the Capitol. The tradition symbolizes the peaceful transfer of power that is a hallmark of American government.

THE INSIDE STORY

James Monroe's 1817 inauguration was supposed to have been held in the chambers of the House of Representatives. However, senators demanded that they be allowed to sit in their own velvet chairs from the Senate chambers during the ceremony. This request outraged the members of the House of Representatives, who thought the senators were just trying to show off. They refused to let the senators bring their own seating. The disagreement went on for so long that the ceremony was moved outdoors as a compromise.

Andrew Jackson (left) escorted Martin Van Buren (right) to the Capitol, beginning the tradition and symbolizing a peaceful transition of power.

Franklin Pierce

A MEMORABLE SPEECH

Franklin Pierce was the first and only president to deliver his inaugural address from memory, in 1853.

★ ★ ★ ★

INAUGURAL ADDRESSES

From the beginning, speeches have been a part of inauguration ceremonies. According to some reports, George Washington's hands shook with emotion as he held his handwritten speech and read it to the Senate and House of Representatives after his first inauguration. At the inauguration for his second term in 1793, Washington delivered the shortest inaugural speech of all time. It consisted of just four sentences and 135 words.

Thomas Jefferson used his 1801 inaugural address to make peace with his political opponents. The election of 1800 was the first hotly contested presidential election. The two political parties of that day—the Republicans and the Federalists— had campaigned hard to win the presidency. Even after the election members of the two parties still held hard feelings. Federalist John Adams did not attend the inauguration of his successor, the Republican Jefferson. In his inauguration speech Jefferson reminded Americans that even people who disagreed politically could agree on

Thomas Jefferson

18

John Adams

James Monroe was the first president to give his inaugural address to a public audience.

their love for their country. "We are all Republicans, we are all Federalists," Jefferson declared. Since then, it has become a tradition for outgoing presidents to attend the inauguration of their successors, even when they are political opponents.

The first four presidents delivered their inaugural addresses to Congress. It wasn't until the inauguration of James Monroe in 1817 that a president spoke to a public audience.

Some of the best-remembered inaugural addresses were delivered during times of crisis. Abraham Lincoln was inaugurated as president for the second time in 1865.

19

Abraham Lincoln

The Civil War was coming to a close, and Lincoln urged Americans to come together as a united nation. "Finish the work we are in," he told his audience. "Bind up the nation's wounds."

In 1933, Franklin D. Roosevelt was inaugurated in the middle of a major crisis—the Great Depression. Thousands of Americans had lost their jobs and fallen into poverty. Many worried that American society was coming apart. Roosevelt reassured them: "This great nation will endure as it has endured, will revive and will prosper." He added, "The only thing we have to fear is fear itself."

Inauguration speeches can also inspire entire generations. In 1961, John Kennedy urged Americans, "Ask not what your country can do for you. Ask what you can do for your country." Many responded by volunteering for government agencies such as the Peace Corps or by becoming more involved in political life.

Inauguration speeches can have unintended **consequences**, too. At his inauguration in 1841, William Henry Harrison read the longest speech ever given at an inauguration. It was 10,000 words long. (That's twice as long as this book.) Harrison was interested in ancient history, and he went on at great length about what could be learned from leaders of

20

* * * *

Poet Maya Angelou at Bill Clinton's Inauguration

Poet Robert Frost

the past. Unfortunately, he read the speech in a driving ice storm, wearing no hat, gloves, or scarf. After his inauguration Harrison became ill with pneumonia. Less than a month later, he was dead.

EMERGENCY PRESIDENTS
Nine times vice presidents have had to take on the highest office in the land after the death or **resignation** of the president. In these cases, the new president takes the presidential

★ ★ ★ ★

A HAIRY INAUGURATION

Theodore Roosevelt wore a ring containing a lock of Abraham Lincoln's hair for his inauguration in 1905.

HISTORIC OATH

Sarah T. Hughes became the first woman to administer the presidential oath when she **presided** at Lyndon Johnson's swearing-in.

oath but doesn't give a formal inaugural address. Usually, the new president will make only a few remarks to reassure the people about his intentions as president.

After the 1901 shooting of President William McKinley in Buffalo, New York, the vice president, Theodore Roosevelt, rushed from his vacation home to join the wounded president. McKinley died before Roosevelt could reach Buffalo. When he finally arrived, Roosevelt took the presidential oath of office in a private mansion with a group of reporters looking on. Knowing that the reporters would tell the world what he said that day, Roosevelt wanted to get his words exactly right. Secretary of War Elihu Root suggested to Roosevelt that he

Lyndon Johnson takes the presidential oath on Air Force One as Jacqueline Kennedy (right) looks on.

22

John Tyler

promise to continue McKinley's policies and to work for peace and prosperity. Roosevelt liked Root's suggestion so much that he used it almost word for word. Roosevelt said, "In this hour of deep and terrible national **bereavement**, I wish to state that it shall be my aim to continue absolutely unbroken the policy of President McKinley for the peace, prosperity, and the honor of our beloved country."

On November 22, 1963, President John Kennedy was shot and killed by an **assassin** in Dallas. His vice president, Lyndon Johnson, became president upon Kennedy's death. Within minutes of Kennedy's death, Johnson boarded Air

Force One, the president's airplane, at the Dallas airport. In the cabin of the airplane he took the presidential oath. Federal judge Sarah Hughes had rushed to the airport to preside over the emergency ceremony. On board the plane, aides looked for a Bible that could be used in the ceremony. All they could find was a small prayer book. With one hand on the prayer book and Kennedy's wife Jacqueline looking on, Johnson took his oath. When the new president's plane returned to Washington, he spoke to the shocked and grief-stricken American people. "We have suffered a loss that cannot be weighed," he said.

"I will do my best. That is all I can do. I ask for your help—and God's."

In 1974, Vice President Gerald R. Ford became president after Richard Nixon resigned in **disgrace.** Nixon was accused of widespread wrongdoing as president, and the nation's confidence in its leaders was shaken. Ford took the presidential oath in the East Room of the White House on August 9, 1974. "I assume the presidency under extraordinary circumstances," Ford said afterward. "This is an hour that troubles our minds and hurts our hearts."

When Calvin Coolidge became president after Warren Harding's death, he made a shorter statement. Asked by someone if he was ready for his new job, Coolidge said, "I think I can swing it."

President Richard M. Nixon

James Madison hosted the first official inaugural ball held in his honor.

PARADES AND PARTIES

After the serious business of oaths and speeches come the parades and parties. The first official inaugural **ball** was held in honor of James Madison, who became the fourth president in 1809. Crowds of people made their way into the ballroom of Long's Hotel in Washington for the dance. The crowd became so thick that dancers began to demand some fresh air be let into the ballroom. Unfortunately, the windows were painted shut, so the glass had to be shattered.

The ball thrown for James Buchanan's inauguration in 1857 was among the most **elaborate** ever. It was held in a building constructed especially for the occasion at a cost of $15,000. The walls were painted red, white, and blue. The ceiling was covered with sparkling gold stars. Six thousand people attended the ball, so large quantities of food and drink were needed. Chefs prepared 75 hams, 500 quarts of chicken salad, and 1,200 quarts of ice cream. The centerpiece of the party was a four-foot-high cake.

The ball for Ulysses S. Grant's 1873 inauguration was not as successful. It was held in a tent outside the White House, which proved to be a bad idea when the temperature dropped below zero. One trumpet player's lips froze to his horn. Caged birds in the tent froze to death, and guests wore their overcoats while dancing.

Over the years, more and more parties and dances have been added to the Inauguration Day schedule. Two balls were given for Martin Van Buren's inauguration in 1837 and three for William Henry Harrison's in 1841. John F. Kennedy's inauguration in 1961 was marked by five balls. In 2000 there were nine balls for George W. Bush.

Madison also began the tradition of parading from the Capitol to the president's house. (It was not yet called the White House.) Most recent presidents have made the trip in a limousine, stopping along the way to get out and greet the people gathered to watch his procession. In 1977, Jimmy Carter became the first president to walk the entire route from the Capitol to the White House after the inauguration.

A long line of marching bands and floats follow the president to the White House. Beginning with Grover

The menu at Abraham Lincoln's inaugural ball in 1865

Cleveland in 1884, it became a tradition for presidents to review the parade from a grandstand outside the White House. Thirty-five thousand people marched in Theodore Roosevelt's 1905 parade. They included members of the Rough Riders, Roosevelt's cavalry regiment from the Spanish-American War. Herbert Hoover's 1929 inauguration parade was the first to include airplanes. John F. Kennedy's parade featured nuclear missiles mounted on trucks.

There was no parade for Thomas Jefferson in 1801. He disliked much of the grand ceremony enjoyed by his **predecessors,** George Washington and John Adams. Before his inauguration Jefferson insisted on walking alone from his hotel to the Capitol. He took the presidential oath at the Capitol and then strolled back to his hotel to have supper. His plain inauguration was a far cry from the elaborate spectacles that would follow. In fact, his inauguration was the first to be held in Washington, D.C., which had just become the nation's capital. At the time, the city resembled one big construction site. Everywhere new buildings stood half-finished. Even the Capitol was unfinished at the

President Dwight D. Eisenhower and Vice President Richard M. Nixon watch the inaugural parade from a grandstand outside the White House.

time of Jefferson's inauguration. Many of Washington's streets were little more than muddy paths dotted with tree stumps. It was hardly a setting for a grand parade.

The celebration at Andrew Jackson's 1829 inauguration is remembered for how quickly it spun out of control. Jackson was immensely popular, a hero of the War of 1812. So many people had gathered outside the Capitol before his inauguration that he could not make his way through the crowd. Instead, Jackson climbed over a fence and entered the Capitol by a back door. After taking the oath of office, Jackson gave a party at the White House, which had been opened to the public. He climbed atop a brilliant white horse and led the crowd in a parade to the White House.

In 1985, Ronald Reagan was inaugurated indoors due to the extremely cold weather.

When they arrived, throngs of Jackson supporters poured into the house to shake hands with the new president. They trampled on chairs and muddied expensive rugs. So many people pushed close to Jackson that he moved outside to escape. Finally, White House workers moved the food and drink outside to the White House lawn. The crowd followed, and further damage to the White House was avoided.

INAUGURAL WEATHER

Snow, cold, and rain sometimes disrupt inaugurations. In 1821, a snowstorm forced James Monroe's second inauguration indoors. The same thing happened in 1833 at Andrew Jackson's second inauguration. An ice storm did not keep William Henry Harrison from reading his lengthy inaugural address. However, the icy weather may have contributed to his death of pneumonia a month later. Cold weather made some of Franklin D. Roosevelt's advisers want to cancel his second inauguration in 1937. However, Roosevelt noticed that crowds continued to gather to watch the ceremony, even in the cold. He decided that if they could stand the cold, so could he. The inauguration went on as planned.

In 1985 temperatures dipped below zero for Ronald Reagan's second inauguration. His swearing-in was moved inside the Capitol. The marching bands that would have paraded down Pennsylvania Avenue instead marched indoors at a nearby arena.

Bill Clinton taking the oath for his second term of office

TECHNOLOGY AND INAUGURATIONS

The only people who saw George Washington's first inauguration were the members of Congress, who gathered in Federal Hall. Over the years technology has helped deliver the words and images of the inauguration to more and more people. In 1809, James Madison's first inaugural address was published in newspapers across the country. In 1845,

* * * *

James K. Polk spoke while inventor Samuel Morse sat alongside him tapping out Polk's words on his revolutionary new telegraph machine. The first inauguration to be photographed was James Buchanan's in 1857. The first to be televised was Harry Truman's in 1949. Today people all over the world watch inaugurations live on television. William Clinton's second inauguration in 1997 was groundbreaking because it was the first one to be broadcast live over the Internet.

TRAVELING TO INAUGURATIONS

Before airplanes and automobiles made travel easier in the twentieth century, getting to a presidential inauguration could be difficult. For presidents in the 1800s, getting to Washington usually involved long trips by stagecoach, horseback, and steamship.

Samuel Morse's invention of the telegraph made it possible to quickly deliver news of James K. Polk's inauguration.

President James K. Polk

★ ★ ★ ★

William Henry Harrison was the first president to take a train to Washington for his 1841 inauguration. The train carried him from Frederick, Maryland to Washington. But before he could board the train, Harrison had to travel the old-fashioned way. He traveled by steamboat from his home in Ohio to Pittsburgh. In Pittsburgh, he switched to a stagecoach, which took him to Frederick, Maryland. There he caught the train to Washington.

Abraham Lincoln's trip from Springfield, Illinois to Washington in 1861 was filled with danger. The United States was on the brink of Civil War and some Southern sympathizers had threatened to kill Lincoln. Private detectives hired to protect the president-elect even found explosives aboard one train. Still, Lincoln refused to change his travel plans. In the railroad station of his hometown of Springfield, he said goodbye to his neighbors. "To this place, and the kindness of these people, I owe everything," Lincoln said. "I now leave, not knowing when or whether ever I may return." Lincoln made it safely to Harrisburg, Pennsylvania. There he finally agreed to take a secret route into Washington to avoid danger. He changed into a long black overcoat and boarded a special train that carried him to the capital earlier than expected.

In 1993, William Clinton followed the path of a previous president to get to Washington. He and vice president-elect Al Gore met in Charlottesville, Virginia, the former home of Thomas Jefferson. From there, Clinton and Gore boarded a bus and followed the route Jefferson traveled to Washington.

President William Henry Harrison traveled to Washington by stagecoach and steamship. Before the invention of the automobile and the airplane, presidential travel was very slow.

Rutherford B. Hayes

ARGUING ABOUT ELECTIONS

Presidential elections can provoke bitter feelings that affect inaugurations. For example, in 1860 several Southern states had vowed to leave the Union if Abraham Lincoln was elected president. After his election his aides feared that someone might try to kill Lincoln before he could be inaugurated. On inauguration day, U.S. Army **sharpshooters** were stationed on rooftops along Lincoln's route to the Capitol to protect him. Still, Lincoln rode to the Capitol in an open carriage. Once there, he stood exposed outside the Capitol to deliver his inauguration speech. "We are not enemies, but friends," he told the people of the South. But within a month, the Civil War was on. Lincoln led the nation through the four-year-long war, but he was assassinated in 1865.

In 1877, Rutherford B. Hayes took his presidential oath in private two days before the official ceremony because of threats made against his life. Hayes had been declared the winner of one of the closest presidential elections of all time. In fact, more people voted for his opponent than for Hayes. Still, a special election **commission** named Hayes president-elect.

The banner promoting Rutherford B. Hayes's opponent Sam Tilden. Some newspapers at the time declared Tilden the winner, even though Hayes was eventually named president.

For weeks following election day in 2000, supporters of George W. Bush and Al Gore still disagreed about who really had won that election. More Americans voted for Gore, but Bush appeared to be winning the Electoral Col-

President George W. Bush

38

lege vote. It wasn't until the U.S. Supreme Court weighed in on the matter that the election was finally decided. Bush was inaugurated on January 20, 2001. After the ceremony one of the first people to shake his hand was Al Gore.

Presidential candidate and former vice president Al Gore

INAUGURAL FIRSTS

1789—George Washington sets the precedent of saying, "So help me God" after taking the Oath of Office.

1801—Thomas Jefferson becomes the first president inaugurated in Washington, D.C.

1809—The United States Marine Corps Band makes its first performance at an inauguration.

1825—John Quincy Adams becomes the first president sworn into office wearing long pants.

1837—Floats appear in the inaugural parade for the first time at Martin Van Buren's inauguration.

1865—African-Americans march in an inaugural parade for the first time at Abraham Lincoln's second inauguration.

1881—James Garfield's mother becomes the first woman to attend her son's inauguration.

1909—First Lady Helen Taft is the first to ride with her husband from the Capitol to the White House.

1921—Warren G. Harding becomes the first president to ride to and from his inauguration in a car.

1925—William Taft is the first former president to administer the oath of office to an incoming president (Calvin Coolidge).

1961—At John F. Kennedy's inauguration, poet Robert Frost reads one of his compositions, the first time a poet takes part in an inauguration.

1965—Lyndon Johnson becomes the first president to use a bullet-proof limousine at his inauguration.

1977—Jimmy Carter walks from the Capitol to the White House after the Inauguration, the first president to do so.

2001—George H.W. Bush is the first former president to watch the inauguration of his son (George W. Bush).

41

Glossary

administered—managed some task or duty

assassin—a person who murders another person or tries to murder another person, sometimes out of a misguided commitment to a cause

ball—a kind of party or gathering at which people dance

bereavement—the process of mourning; sadness at the loss of a loved one

ceremony—formal events that mark or celebrate an important day

Chief Justice of the United States—the principal judge of the U.S. Supreme Court

commission—a group of persons given an important task to perform, or decision to make

consequences—things that happen as the result of some action

disgrace—shame or dishonor

elaborate—grand and complicated

inauguration—a ceremony marking the beginning
    of a person's term in an important job

oath—a promise to tell the truth or perform a certain task

portico—a kind of porch supported by columns and
    attached to a building

predecessors—people who do a job before another person

presided—supervised or was in charge of

president-elect—a person who has been elected
    president, but who has not yet taken office

resignation—the act of leaving a job or position
    in government

sharpshooters—soldiers or police officers able to fire
    weapons with great accuracy

tardy—late

Timeline:U.S. Presidential

1789	1801	1809	1817	1841	1861	1877

George Washington is inaugurated as first president on April 30.

Thomas Jefferson becomes the first president to be sworn in at the new capital city of Washington, D.C.

James Madison hosts the first inaugural ball.

James Monroe becomes first president to deliver an inaugural address to a public audience.

William Henry Harrison delivers the longest inauguration speech in history, lasting 90 minutes.

Abraham Lincoln is inaugurated as the nation prepares for Civil War.

Rutherford B. Hayes takes oath of office after a special commission names him president.

Inaugurations

1925	1933	1937	1949	1961	1963	2001
Calvin Coolidge's inauguration is the first to be broadcast on radio.	Twentieth Amendment to the Constitution changes Inauguration Day to January 20.	Franklin D. Roosevelt becomes the first president inaugurated on January 20.	Harry Truman's inauguration is the first to be televised.	John F. Kennedy issues a call for national service in his inauguration speech.	Lyndon Johnson takes the oath of office on board Air Force One after John F. Kennedy's death.	George W. Bush is inaugurated on January 20, after the U.S. Supreme Court resolves election disputes in his favor.

To Find Out More

BOOKS

Bausum, Ann. *Our Country's Presidents.* National Geographic Society, 2001.

Bendat, Jim. *Democracy's Big Day: The Inauguration of Our President.* Writer's Club, Ltd., 2000.

St. George, Judith. *So You Want to Be President?* New York: Philomel Books, 2000.

ONLINE SITES

Inauguration 2001
http://www.pbs.org/newshour/inauguration
Presidential inauguration history from PBS.

Inaugural 2001
http://www.2001inaugural.com/
Official Web site of the forty-third inauguration.

Index

Bold numbers indicate illustrations.

Administered, 15, 22, 41, 42

assassin, 23, 42

Ball, 26–27, 42

bereavement, 23, 42

Bush, G.W., 12, 27, 38–39, 41

Ceremony, 10, 11, 42, 43

Chief Justice of U.S., 15, 42

Clinton, Bill, 21, **32**, 33, 35

commission, 36, 39, 42, 44

consequences, 20, 42

Constitution, 6–9, 11–12, 15

Coolidge, C., 15, **16**, 25, 41

Disgrace, 25, 42

Elaborate, 26, 28, 42

Electoral College, 12, 38–39

Harding, W., 15, **16**, 25, 40

Harrison, W.H., 10, 20–21, 23, 27, 31, 34

Hayes, R.B., **36**, 37

Inaugural addresses, 9, 10, 14, 16, 18–21, 32, 44–45

inauguration, defined, 43

Jackson, A., 17, **17**, 29, 31

Jefferson, T., **18**, 18–19, 28–29, 34, 40

Johnson, Lyndon B., 10, 22–25, 41

Kennedy, John F., 10, **14**, 15, 20–24, 27–28, 41, **41**

Lame Duck Amendment, 12–13, 45

Lincoln, Abraham, 19–20, **20**, 27, 34–35, 36–37, 40

Madison, J., **26**, 26–27, 32

Monroe, J., 17, 19, **19**, 31

Nixon, Richard, 25, **25**

Oath, presidential, 8, 15, 43

Portico, 16, 43

predecessor, 16–17, 19, 28, 43

presided, 22, 24, 43

president-elect, 10, 13, 15, 16–17, 35, 37, 43

Resignation, 21, 25, 43

Roosevelt, F., 13, 16, 20, 31

Roosevelt, Theodore, 22–23, 28

Sharpshooter, 36–37, 43

Tardy, 12, 43

Van Buren, M., 17, **17**, 27, 40

Washington, George, 3-5, 7-9, 10–12, 15–16, 18, 28, 32, 40

About the Author

Andrew Santella writes for magazines and newspapers, including *Gentlemen's Quarterly* and the *New York Times Book Review*. He is the author of several Children's Press books, including *The Battle of the Alamo* and *Mount Rushmore*.